The Usb[...]
Poc[...]
Puzzle
Book

Written by
Alex Frith and
Sarah Courtauld

Designed by
Zoe Wray

Illustrated by
Peter Allen,
Agostino Traini,
Benedetta Giaufret
and Enrica Rusinà

Start here.

2

Can you help Wally the waiter find his way to the man ringing the bell?

3

Which gnome has hooked a fish? And which gnome has hooked an old boot?

5

There are two shifty people on this train: one passenger who didn't buy a ticket, and an undercover spy. See if you can identify them.

Renumber these fashions to put them in historical order, starting with the earliest.

Help the fly escape from this web maze. Mind the threads - they're very sticky.

Fill in the grid with these four insects. Each row, column, and 4-square box must contain one of each.

 Ladybird Bill

 Butterfly Bertha

 Alexander Ant

 Anabella Bee

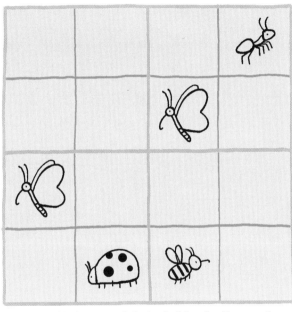

You can write the names in instead of drawing if you prefer.

One of these fish is different from all the others. Can you find it?

This astronaut has a camera on his helmet.

12

Which screen shows the view from the camera on the astronaut's helmet?

Are there more twinkling blue stars... ...or round red comets?

Which flying saucer is different from all the others?

It's the opening match of the basketball season...

...can you spot eight differences between these two scenes?

Can you find four athletes wearing the wrong clothes?

18

Can you find six athletes holding the wrong equipment?

19

These animals all live in cold places, except for one.
Can you see which animal does not belong?

Here are some inventions in the history of writing. Two are in the wrong order - which two?

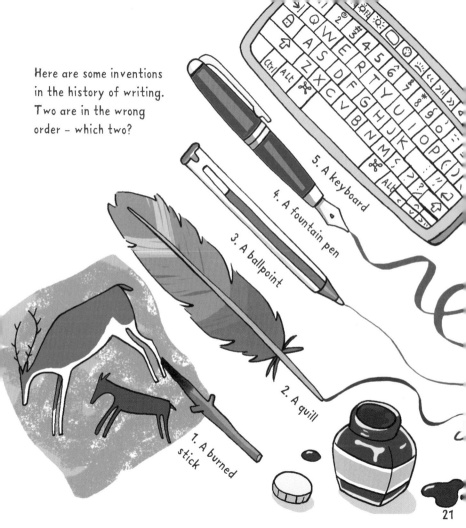

5. A keyboard

4. A fountain pen

3. A ballpoint

2. A quill

1. A burned stick

21

Tessa is trying to see these four views through her telescope, but she can only find three. Which view can't she see?

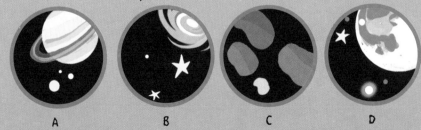

A   B   C   D

The letters in this serpent's body spell out seven snake names.
Can you identify them all?

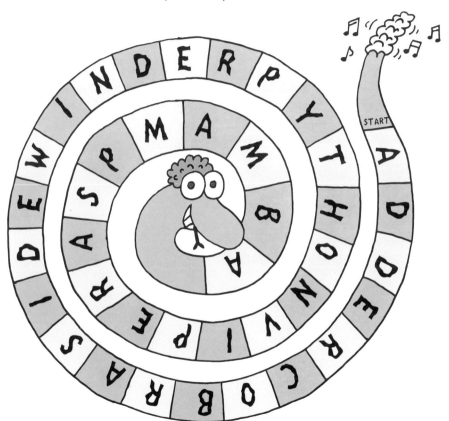

The Three Billys have been caught in the middle of a robbery.
Can you spot which sheriff has caught the swag bag,
and which sheriff has caught Billy The Kid?

BANK

Sheriff Truman

Sheriff Whataman

Billy the Grandpa

Sheriff Justaman

Sheriff Wiseman

Billy the Dad

Billy the Kid

SWAG

One of these owls is different from all the others. Can you find it?

All the words hidden in this
grid have an 'L' in them.
Can you find them?

L̶A̶M̶P̶	LARVA	LOOK
L̶A̶K̶E̶	LARGE	EQUAL
GOAL	LEMUR	LADLE
VELVET	KOALA	LOAF

Clue: the words can be read from
left to right or up and down.

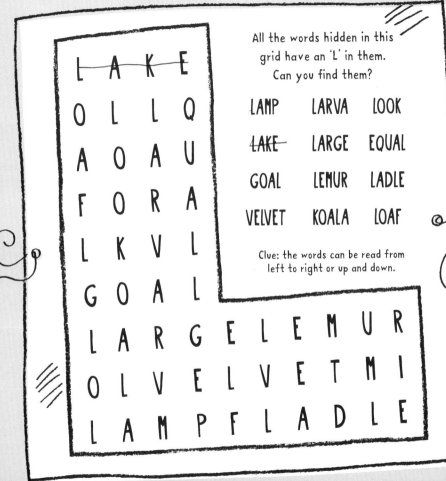

L A K E
O L L Q
A O A U
F O R A
L K V L
G O A L
L A R G E L E M U R
O L V E L V E T M I
L A M P F L A D L E

28

Which ghost is different from the rest?

If **12 thrushes** can eat **6 packets** of bird seed,

and

6 parakeets can eat **4 packets**,

how many packets can **4 thrushes** and **3 parakeets** eat?

Monsieur Le Boeuf needs some help to make his Grand Burgers.
How many can he can he make with these ingredients?

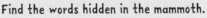

Find the words hidden in the mammoth.

CAVEMAN   WOOLLY

PAINTS   MAMMOTH

TOOTH   FURS

TIGER   TOOLS

HAIRY   TRACKER

HUNTER   SPEAR

TUSK   FIRE

Clue: the words can be read left to right, or up and down.

33

Two of the rabbits in this garden are identical. Can you spot them?

Follow the letters up the trunk
and along the branches of this tree.
How many words can you spell out?

This scene shows a busy medieval town. Look for the following:

 A windmill

 People fighting with swords

 A boat with four people on board

 Two cats

 People hanging up clothes to dry

 Nine pigs

 Two people emptying buckets

Dozy

Mick

Tich

Fill in the grid with these four clowns. Each row, column, and 4-square box must contain one of each.

Beaky

If you prefer, you can write their names instead of drawing their faces.

38

Who is flying the butterfly kite?

Stan

Gerry

Len

Marv

Denny

Which boat has Pirate Pettigrew untied from its mooring?

E

Pirate Pettigrew

F

41

Look for the
following:

A mountain
climber with
a green hat

A pair of
toadstools

A rabbit

An abominable
snowman

An upside-down
snowboarder

A frozen lake

A helicopter

A mouse

42

Where will each ball land?

These are bacteria.

These are not bacteria.

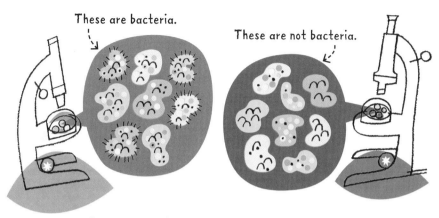

How many bacteria can you see in this sample?

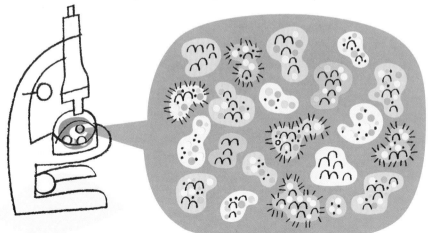

45

World famous art thief, Sally Spiderfingers, has boasted that she is going to steal one of these famous paintings. Read this newspaper article to find a clue that'll help you discover which painting she is after.

Famous paintings to go on show

A. Sunflowers

B. The Scream

C. The Mona Lis

On show for the first time in the same exhibiton are three fabulous masterpieces. Sunflowers, by Vincent van Gogh, The Scream by Edvard Munch, and Leonardo da Vinci's Mona Lisa, also known as La Joconde.

The security in place at the museum is top

notch – it's as tight as it has ever been. A spokesperson for the security team said:

"Even the most skilled cat burglar in the world couldn't penetrate our sophisticated laser screen.

We have guards posted on the roof and even in the sewers that lead into the gallery bathroom!"

However, police have warned that a notorious art thief has planned to steal one of the three paintings. Superintendent Barden issued this statement, appealing to the public for help:

"Sally is very well connected. She has an insider in several newspapers who is sowing clues into articles including this very one. Look out for dots above the letters. If they spell out words, it definitely means something. Be sure to report any clues, however weird or wild, to your local police station."

The question remains: which world famous, beautiful artwork will this jaw-droppingly cunning scoundrel try to steal?

Which length of hair will lead the knight to the real princess?

Count the insects.
Are there more butterflies... ...or bees?

There are five invisible ghosts hard at work in this kitchen.
Can you guess where they all are?

51

Find the two matching cars.

What is the correct historical sequence for these four scenes?

Try to match each musician to his or her instrument.

...can you spot eight differences between the two scenes?

All these notes about missing animals have letters missing. But which of them was written using the old fashioned typewriter on the left?

C

On_ y_llo_ b_tt_rfly _ith r_d p_rpl_ and bl__ spots. R__ard off_r_d.

B

On_ larg_ gr__n frog. Last s__n ho__ing ov_r th_ villag_ gr__n. _l_as_ h_l_!

A

Pin_ and lilac mayfly. Li__s lav_nd_r and r_d ros_s. Answ_rs to th_ nam_ Mar_.

There are six invisible witches in this lair.
Can you guess where they all are?

Oops! The names for these statues of Ancient Greek gods are all in the wrong places. Use the clues to decide which name belongs to which statue.

Hermes is the god of speed. **Ares** is the god of war.

Demeter

Ares

Athena

Zeus is the god of thunder and lightning.   Athena is the goddess of wisdom.

Demeter is the goddess of the harvest.   Poseidon is the god of the sea.

Look for these words, hidden in the chemist's flask:

BURNER	SMOKE
BANG	GOGGLES
FIZZ	PETRI
TIN	DISH
FIRE	REACT
TUBE	IRON
FLAME	ACID

Clue: the words can be read side to side, up and down, diagonally, or even back to front.

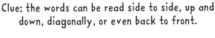

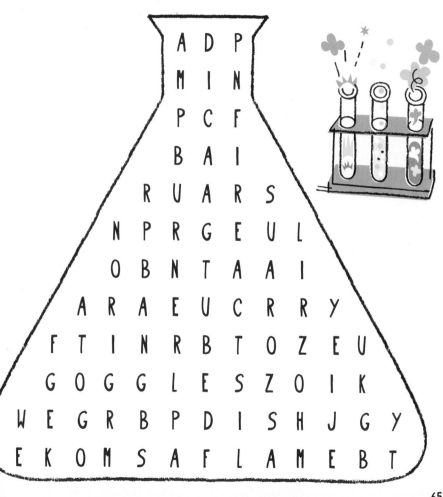

A D P
M I N
P C F
B A I
R U A R S
N P R G E U L
O B N T A A I
A R A E U C R R Y
F T I N R B T O Z E U
G O G G L E S Z O I K
W E G R B P D I S H J G Y
E K O M S A F L A M E B T

Only two of these zebras are identical. Can you find them?

Clue: look at the legs and tails.

Which vine is safe to swing from?

Can you find the matching medallion?

1

2

3

These are **Martians.** They all have spots
and antennae on their heads.

These are **Venusians.** They all have three legs,
but none of them has antennae.

How many **Martians** and **Venusians** can you see at this party?

69

Which butterfly comes next in the sequence?

In a tug of war, if 3 mice are evenly matched with 1 cat...

...and 1 cat + 2 mice are evenly matched with 1 dog...

...who will win when a dog and a cat take on 5 mice?

71

How many cupcakes  have fallen out of Red Riding Hood's basket?

Find all these words hidden in the pan.

SIZZLE	SOUP	PARSLEY
SAUCE	CRUNCHY	TORTILLA
SLICE	CHOP	BAKE
OVEN	WHISK	PIZZA
EGGS	SWEET	STIR
OMELETTE	APPLE	STEW

Clue: the words can be read side to side,
up and down, or diagonally.

```
      P A B P Q
  Z O T Z S A B Y H O
  A S I Z Z L E K A T M C
O S P A Z I I G S E N E R S
V T S O U P C G I L T L U T
M E C V T C E S H P G E N I
S W E E T H E O W P Z T C R
E U B N C O V M A A F T H E
  I S Q U P P A R S L E Y
    T O R T I L L A
```

The three sentences written on this stone tablet all say the same thing using a different alphabet.

THE ΣΠHINX
KNO6N AΣ YOΓ
6AΣ MAΔE ΦPOM
ΞET BΛAΨK ΘΘAPTZ

THE SPHINX KNOWN AS
YOG WAS MADE FROM
JET BLACK QUARTZ

τηε σπηινχ κνοφν
ασ υογ φασ μαδε
φρομ ξετ βλαψκ
θθαρτχ

Use the tablet to crack the codes, and reveal the hidden messages.

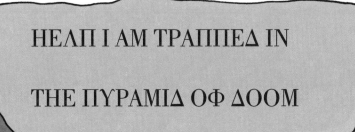

ΗΕΛΠ Ι ΑΜ ΤΡΑΠΠΕΔ ΙΝ

ΤΗΕ ΠΥΡΑΜΙΔ ΟΦ ΔΟΟΜ

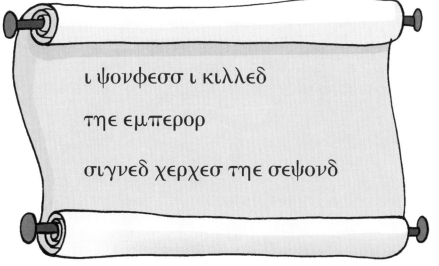

ι ψονφεσσ ι κιλλεδ

τηε εμπερορ

σιγνεδ χερχεσ τηε σεψονδ

Which shoe sole matches the shoe print found at this crime scene?

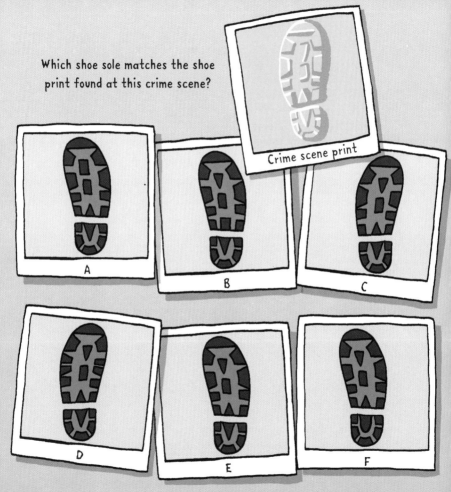

Crime scene print

A

B

C

D

E

F

Find the two identical robots.

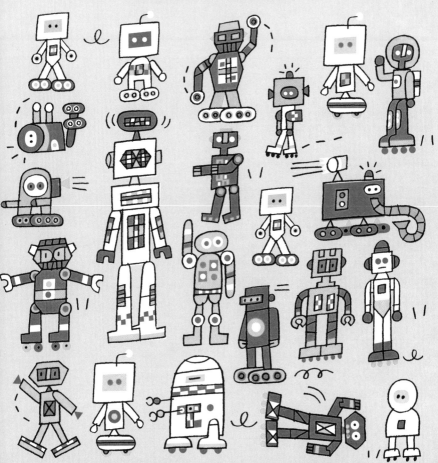

4 minutes

FINISH

1 minute

4 minutes

83

Look at the footprints on the right. Can you guess which of these creatures did not walk through the mud?

A The raven

B The hiker

C The yak

D The duck

E The tiger

F The monster

84

What shape comes next in this sequence?

is it....

A   B   C

The artist has hidden a deliberate mistake in this story about a bicycle accident. Can you find it?

88

Which are there more of in this zoo – zebras or penguins?

Follow these instructions to find the **hidden treasure** on the map.
You can travel through forests and across mountains,
but you can only cross rivers using bridges.

Every time you
come to a bridge,
cross it.

Always go west
to escape from
a dragon.

Always turn
north when you
find a castle.

Always turn
east when you
find a church.

Always turn south to
escape from an ogre.

Is the treasure buried:

In the cave?

Under the stone circle?

In the well?

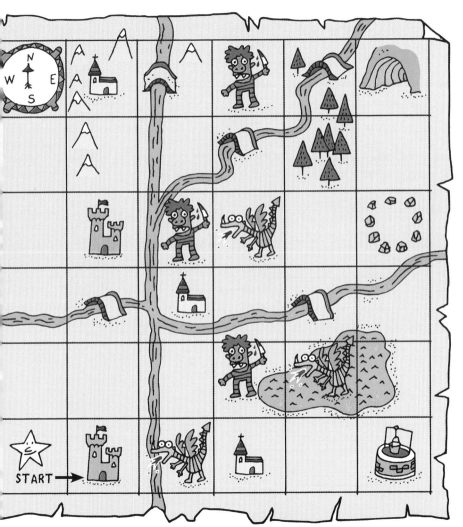

START →

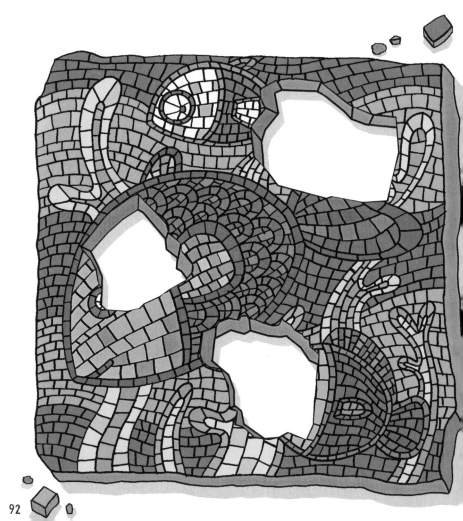

Archeologists have just discovered this ancient mosaic, and it needs to be put back together. But which of these pieces does not fit onto the mosaic?

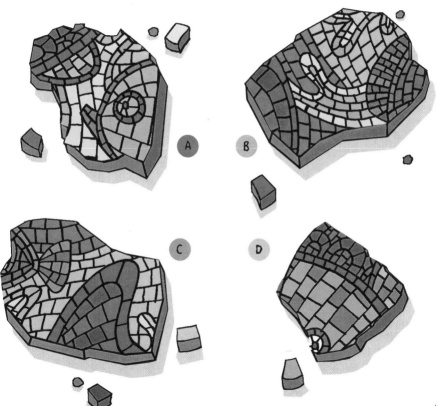

A

B

C

D

How many complete monsters can you build from these body parts?

95

Can you guide the plane to the airport without passing through any clouds?

START

Put these pictures in the right order to tell
the story of a boy's day out at the funfair.

Follow the trail of bottles to read a message from the man on the island.

Spot six things that don't belong on this fruit and vegetable stall.

99

Can you find the book that the young wizard is looking for?

These sheep keep fighting and need to be on their own.
Can you draw four straight fences to isolate them all?

Which team has the most knights - the red team or the blue team?

See if you can find all these words,
hidden in the sail of the pirate ship.

SKULL	CROSS	BONES
YARGH	CUTLASS	SAIL
HOOK	SWASH	SWIM
SEA	BUCKLE	RUM
MONSTER	CHEST	SHOT
RUSTY	PLANK	COIN

Clue: the words can be read side to side,
up and down, or diagonally.

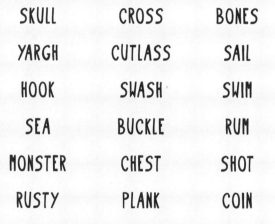

Can you find nine modern things in this historical banquet scene?

109

START

Help the pirate row to the treasure.
Watch out for sharks, volcanoes and cannon fire!

110

Fill in the grid with these four fruits.
Each row, column, and 4-square box
must contain one of each.

Escape from the Gingerbread house by following
the trail of cookies to Grandma's house.
Avoid the red cookies - they are burning hot.

Start here.

Gingerbread
house

Grandma's house

113

Answers

Pages 2-3

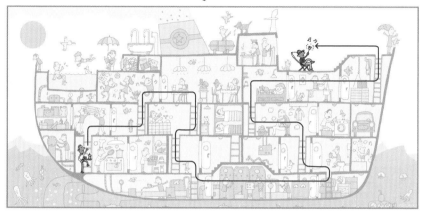

Pages 4-5

Gnome E has hooked the fish.
Gnome D has hooked the old boot.

Pages 6-7

The fare dodger is marked in blue.
The spy is marked in red.

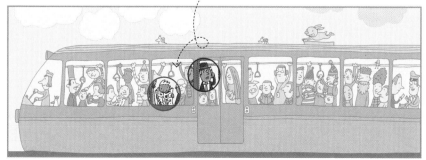

Page 8

5 — 1 — 3
2 — 6 — 4

(Ancient Egyptian princess, Medieval European
princess, 17th century French courtier,
Victorian lady, 1920s flapper girl, 1970s punk.)

Page 9

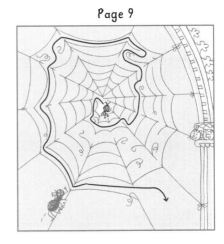

Page 10

Page 11

Pages 12-13
Screen D shows the correct view.

Page 14
There are 4 blue stars, and 5 red comets.

Page 15

Page 16-17

Pages 18-19

Page 20
The snake is the creature that does not belong.

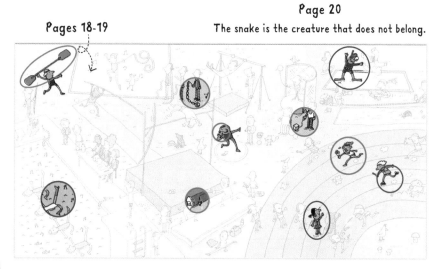

Page 21

The fountain pen should come before the ballpoint pen in the sequence.

Page 22

View D is not visible.

Page 23

The seven snakes are: adder, cobra, sidewinder, python, viper, asp, mamba.

Page 26

Sheriff Whataman has lassoed the loot.

Sherriff Justaman has caught Billy the Kid.

Page 27

Pages 24-25

117

Page 28

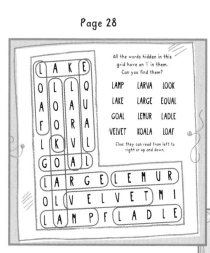

All the words hidden in this grid have an 'l' in them. Can you find them?

LAMP   LARVA   LOOK

LAKE   LARGE   EQUAL

GOAL   LEMUR   LADLE

VELVET   KOALA   LOAF

Clue: they can read from left to right or up and down.

Page 29

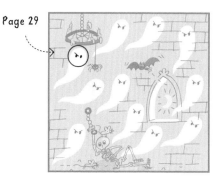

Page 30

The thrushes eat two packets and the parakeets eat two packets - making four in total.

Page 31

Each Grand Burger needs a top and bottom bun, a slice of tomato, a burger and a lettuce leaf. So Mr Le Boeuf can make four complete burgers.

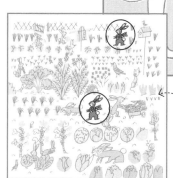

Pages 32-33

Page 34

Page 35

There are six words to find: sprightly, springboard, springtime, springbok, sprinkling, sprinkler.

Pages 36-37

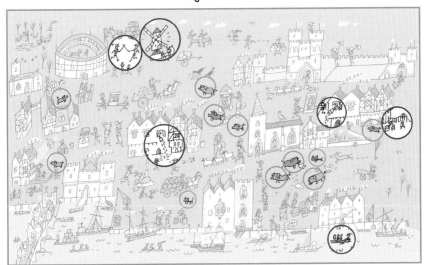

Page 38

Page 39

Marv is flying the
butterfly kite.

Pages 40-41
Pirate Pettigrew
has untangled
Boat E.

Page 44

The red ball will land at point C.
The yellow ball will land at point A.
The green ball will land at point B.

Page 45

Bacteria must have green and yellow blobs
inside, and black dots, and black bumps.
They can be hairy.
So there are
10 bacteria
in dish C.

Pages 46-47

The hidden message reads:
"The scream is a fake. I stole the original
last year. Tomorrow I will steal La Joconde."

The article also explains that 'La Joconde' is
another name for the Mona Lisa.

Page 48

Hair C leads to the princess.

Page 49

There are nine butterflies,
but only seven bees.

Pages 50-51

Page 52

Page 53

The correct order is: D B C A
(The time of the dinosaurs, the Crusades, the
first steam train, the present day)

Pages 54-55

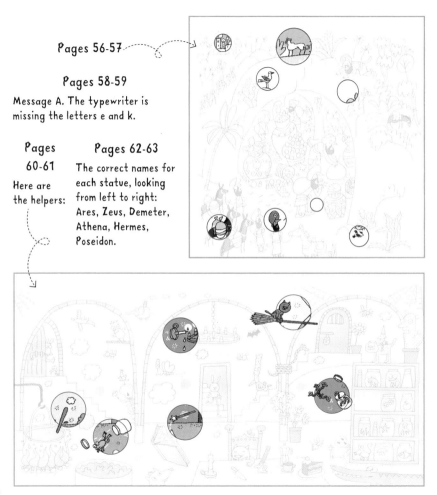

Pages 56-57

Pages 58-59
Message A. The typewriter is missing the letters e and k.

Pages 60-61
Here are the helpers:

Pages 62-63
The correct names for each statue, looking from left to right: Ares, Zeus, Demeter, Athena, Hermes, Poseidon.

Pages 64-65

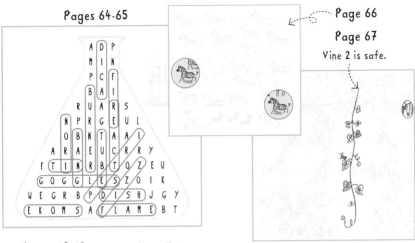

Page 66

Page 67

Vine 2 is safe.

Pages 68-69

There are 8 Martians and 5 Venusians.

Page 71

The dog and cat will win.

Page 70

This is the next butterfly: C

Page 72

Red Riding Hood has dropped nine cupcakes.

Page 73

The windows correspond to the letters on the sheet of paper. Spelling out the letters from the lighted windows reveals the password: leopard.

Pages 74-75

123

Pages 76-77

Here are the
invisible helpers:

Pages 78-79

The messages
read:
"Help I am
trapped in the
pyramid of doom"
"I confess I killed
the Emperor
signed Xerxes
the second"

Page 80

Shoe sole E matches
the print.

Pages 82-83

Steffi will get to the swings in 8 minutes.
Julia and Donald both take 9 minutes.

Pages 84-85

The duck did not walk through the mud.

Page 81

Page 86

This is the next shape:

Page 87

In picture C, the
stripes on the
ball are in the
wrong order.

Page 88

Lucy is eating Nancy's
ice-cream cone.

Page 89

There are 13
penguins but
only 8 zebras.

Pages 90-91

The treasure is in the well.
Here is the path to follow:

Page 96

Pages 92-93

Piece B does not fit the mosaic.

Page 94

Each monster needs a head, legs, a chest, a brain, and two hands. So you can only build three complete monsters.

Page 95

The correct order is: Rocket steam locomotive (early 19th century), Ford Model T car (early 20th century), NASA Space shuttle (late 20th century), Smart car (early 21st century).

Page 97

B, D, C, A

Page 98

Clue: start reading from the bottom. The message reads: PLEASE LEAVE ME ALONE.

Page 99

Page 100

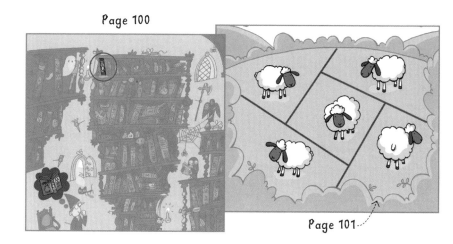

Page 101

Pages 102-103

Pages 104-105

There are 12 knights on the blue team but only 10 knights on the red team.

Pages 106-107

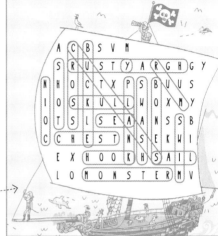

Pages 108-109

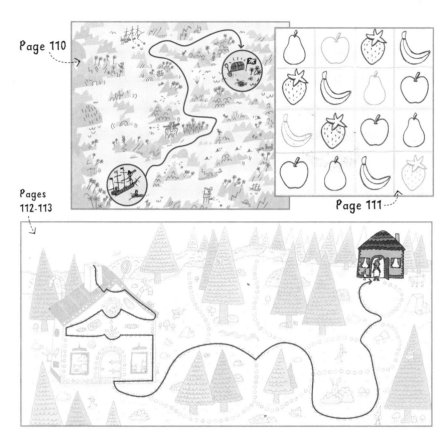

Page 110

Page 111

Pages 112-113